H●CKEY

JENNIFER ANDERSON AND JENNY ELLISON

CANADIAN MUSEUM OF HISTORY
MUSÉE CANADIEN DE L'HISTOIRE

Library and Archives Canada
Cataloguing in Publication

Anderson, Jennifer, author
Hockey / Jennifer Anderson
and Jenny Ellison.

(Souvenir catalogue series,
ISSN 2291-6385; 18)
Issued also in French under the same title.
ISBN 978-1-988282-02-2 (softcover)

1.   Hockey – Canada – History.
I.   Ellison, Jenny, author.
II. Canadian Museum of History,
     issuing body.
III. Title.
IV. Series: Souvenir catalogue series; 18.

GV848.4.C3A63 2017
796.9620971
C2017-900796-3

Published by the
Canadian Museum of History
100 Laurier Street
Gatineau, QC K1A 0M8
historymuseum.ca

Printed and bound in Canada

This work is a souvenir of the exhibition
Hockey, which was developed by the
Canadian Museum of History and presented
in partnership with Pointe-à-Callière,
Montréal Archaeology and History Complex.

Souvenir Catalogue series, 18
ISSN 2291-6385

CONTENTS

////////////////////////////

FOREWORD

////////////////////////

For millions of Canadians, winter means hockey and hockey means everything. Whether it's played in a gigantic arena before thousands of screaming fans, on a frozen pond in rural Canada or on a quiet suburban cul-de-sac, this all-consuming pastime grips the national imagination.

Hockey traces the evolution of Canadians' love affair with the sport, from its origins in the outdoor stick-and-ball games of Indigenous Peoples and European settlers, through the development of amateur hockey leagues and into the current era of professional hockey as multimedia spectacle.

This generously illustrated souvenir catalogue introduces us to the luminaries who played important roles in shaping the game along the way. We meet not only star players — from Howie Morenz and Maurice "Rocket" Richard to Hayley Wickenheiser and Sidney Crosby — but also the supporting cast of coaches, broadcasters and grassroots game changers who have been essential to the history of hockey.

Making stops at landmark events such as Montréal's 1955 Richard Riot and Paul Henderson's winning goal in the 1972 Canada–U.S.S.R. Summit Series, **Hockey** also casts its gaze on longer term trends in the game's evolution. It details the advances in equipment technology — skates, sticks, goalie masks, the specialized equipment used in sledge hockey — that have propelled the game forward. It considers the hockey iconography, such as team jerseys and the coveted Stanley Cup, that has stoked the passion of fans. And it revisits whimsical offshoots of the game — table hockey, Roch Carrier's beloved book *The Hockey Sweater*, souvenir collectibles — that have also contributed to the hockey mystique.

Through one-of-a-kind artifacts and historical photos, **Hockey** recreates the excitement that emerged from the depths of the Canadian winter and continues to thrive in communities across the country. Detailed and evocative, it shows why hockey holds pride of place in the hearts of Canadians.

Jean-Marc Blais
Director General
Canadian Museum of History

INTRODUCTION

////////////////////////

For Canadians, hockey is more than just a game.
It is a national and personal passion. Regardless
of geography, language, gender, age or
background, Canadians everywhere play hockey.

They watch, read and wear it too. Hockey's
memorable moments are closely connected
to the history of Canada itself.

FROM POND TO ARENA

////////////////////////

From its origins on the outdoor rink to the modern game, hockey grew quickly in popularity, but remains rooted in communities across the country.

EARLIEST KNOWN PHOTO
OF WOMEN PLAYING HOCKEY

Rideau Hall, Ottawa, Ont.
1890

HOW HOCKEY BECAME
CANADA'S GAME

No one knows the origins of hockey. In North America, it evolved from outdoor stick-and-ball games played by both Indigenous Peoples and European settlers. Each of these games had its own set of rules, agreed upon by the participants.

More common in colder climates, hockey was usually played on ice, which led to the development of skates for faster, more skilled play. Harsh winters and vast expanses of frozen water made Canada a natural home.

EARLY HOCKEY STICK

This is the earliest known hockey stick,
handmade in Canada. A boy named William
"Dilly" Moffatt used it to play hockey on the local
pond. His initials are carved into the blade.

EARLIEST KNOWN HOCKEY STICK

Cape Breton, N.S.
1835–1838

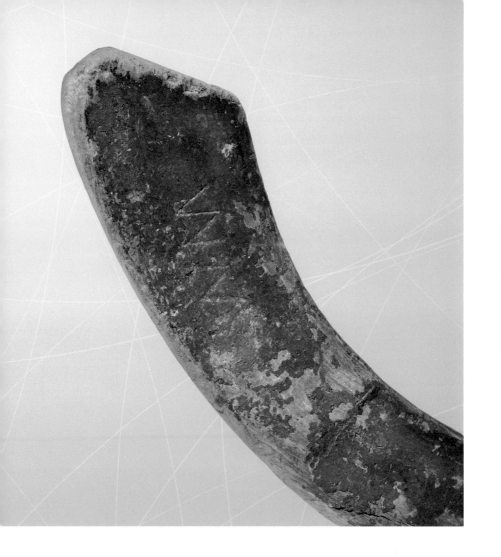

SOUVENIR MEDALLION

Bytown (Ottawa), Ont.
1852

SILVER SHINTY MEDAL

"Shinty" is one of many historical names for what we now call hockey. Hugh Masson kept this souvenir of a match he played at Rideau Hall, Ottawa, in December 1852.

INNOVATIVE SKATE BLADES

In 1865, the Starr Manufacturing Company
revolutionized hockey by offering a blade
that could attach securely to a skating boot.
These blades were affordable and could be
purchased by catalogue.

ACME CLUB SKATES (RIGHT)

Halifax, N.S.
1865

ATLAS SKATES (LEFT) AND ICONIC BOX

Dartmouth, N.S.
1910–1925

HOCKEY MATCH AT McGILL UNIVERSITY

Montréal, Que.
1901

THE GAME GETS ORGANIZED

After hundreds of years of informal or pickup hockey, standardized rules brought teams together on equal terms. Amateur leagues grew rapidly as Canada's rising population and better transportation links made it easier to organize teams, fund skating rinks and travel to play in other towns.

At this time, competitive teams were composed mostly of "gentlemen amateurs" because they could afford to play. The Stanley Cup was first awarded in 1893, to the best amateur hockey team in Canada.

HOCKEY AT THE
MONTRÉAL CARNIVAL

Spectators were thrilled to see the relatively new game of hockey at the Montréal Winter Carnival. The McGill University team won this trophy at the Carnival in 1883.

WINTER CARNIVAL HOCKEY TROPHY

Montréal, Que.
1883

**INTERPROVINCIAL
BANK
CHAMPIONSHIP
TROPHY**

Montréal, Que.
1894

INDUSTRIAL TEAMS

The Bank of Montreal hockey team won this trophy in an interprovincial competition in the 1890s. Then, as now, workplace-based teams competed for honours and bragging rights.

THE STANLEY CUP

In 1892, Lord Stanley — the Governor General of Canada — announced that he would donate a challenge cup to be awarded to the best amateur hockey team in the country. In 1893, the Montreal Amateur Athletic Association team was the first to win the Stanley Cup.

**LORD STANLEY
OF PRESTON**

Ottawa, Ont.
1889

THE GROWTH OF PROFESSIONAL AND AMATEUR LEAGUES

In the early 1900s, amateur teams coexisted with early professional leagues. The best amateur team in the country represented Canada internationally; but increasingly, professional leagues with paid players fed the public's interest in seeing the best teams compete. A growing fan base and the efforts of business promoters resulted in the formation of the National Hockey League (NHL) in November 1917.

EARLY SKATING RINK

Québec, Que.
1894

HOCKEY TRADING CARDS

Distributed by Imperial Tobacco
1910–1911 season

THE NATIONAL HOCKEY ASSOCIATION

One of the first entirely professional leagues was the National Hockey Association (NHA), formed in 1909. These hockey cards, from the first set ever produced, recall the legendary NHA players who transformed the game.

HILDA RANSCOMBE OF THE PRESTON RIVULETTES

Women's hockey clubs attracted huge paying audiences in the 1930s.
The Preston Rivulettes captured four national championships that
decade. Team member Hilda Ranscombe was the best player of the era.
She wore this uniform and these skates.

**RANSCOMBE'S
HOCKEY
UNIFORM
AND SKATES**

Preston, Ont.
1930s

**HILDA
RANSCOMBE**

1930s

THE RCAF FLYERS

St. Moritz Winter
Olympic Games
1948

RCAF FLYERS
HOCKEY SWEATER

Worn in St. Moritz,
Switzerland
1948

THE ROYAL CANADIAN AIR FORCE FLYERS

Wing Commander Hubert Brooks wore this Royal Canadian Air Force (RCAF) Flyers sweater to represent Canada at the 1948 Winter Olympics in St. Moritz, Switzerland. The team won the gold medal.

HOCKEY AS SPECTACULAR ENTERTAINMENT

Professional hockey has evolved from humble origins into sleek, multimedia entertainment. Though there have been other professional leagues since 1917, the NHL remains the pinnacle of professional hockey accomplishment and a complex, billion-dollar corporate enterprise.

MAPLE LEAF GARDENS

Toronto, Ont.
1932

OTTAWA SENATORS VS. BOSTON BRUINS

Ottawa, Ont.
November 15, 2013

HOWIE MORENZ MEMORIAL GAME

Thousands of people paid tribute to Montréal Canadiens player Howie Morenz, following his untimely death from an undetected blood clot in 1937. The memorial game organized in his honour was one of the first all-star games.

HOWIE MORENZ

Member of the Stanley
Cup-winning Montréal
Canadiens

Montréal, Que.
1929–1930 season

MORENZ BUTTON
AND RIBBON

Montréal, Que.
November 2, 1937

MAURICE "ROCKET" RICHARD

A tremendously skilled hockey player, Maurice "Rocket" Richard gained a heroic stature that transcended his on-ice career. By the end of his career, he had become a living legend.

RICHARD'S STANLEY CUP
CHAMPIONSHIP RING

Montréal, Que.
1959

GAME ON!

////////////////////////////

Certain iconic players have had
a tangible influence on the game
and its popularity. This impact is
reflected in the equipment industry,
in advertising and fashion, and
on the backyard rink.

STICKHANDLING

The stick is a hockey player's principal tool, an extension of his or her body that allows puck movement, scoring and defensive finesse. The best early sticks were carved by hand from a single piece of wood. Today's hockey sticks are lightweight marvels of scientific innovation.

Players choose their sticks for comfort and competitive advantage, but their choices affect industry, commerce and popular culture. Endorsement of a hockey stick by a professional player is a financial coup for the manufacturer.

FROM TOP TO BOTTOM:

Sher-Wood stick used to play ball hockey at the
Kandahar Air Field hockey pad in Afghanistan;

Marie-Philip Poulin's stick, used to score the
game-winning goal at the 2010 Winter Olympic Games;

Easton composite stick that Sheldon Souray used
while with the Montréal Canadiens;

George Armstrong's stick from his 1954–1955 season
with the Toronto Maple Leafs;

Wayne Gretzky's signed Titan stick, from his
Edmonton Oilers years;

A stick Ken Dryden used while with the Montréal Canadiens.

SKATING SPEED

Skate blades allow players to execute fast and controlled movements, making hockey one of the quickest and most agile sports. The earliest skaters attached blades to their own boots. This lasted until skates were developed that securely joined blade and boot.

In 1957, after Maurice Richard's Achilles tendon was cut during a game, skate manufacturers added leather safety heels. More recently, blades attached to hockey sledges have made the game more accessible. Innovations continue, with skate design being one of hockey's most competitive fields.

**GEORGE ARMSTRONG,
TORONTO MAPLE LEAFS,
LACING UP HIS SKATES**

Toronto, Ont.
1962

HOCKEY AND THE MAIL-ORDER CATALOGUE

Hockey players endorsed sports equipment sold by mail-order
catalogue, which brought the sport to remote communities across
the country. In the 1950s, Maurice "Rocket" Richard brand skates
like these were popular.

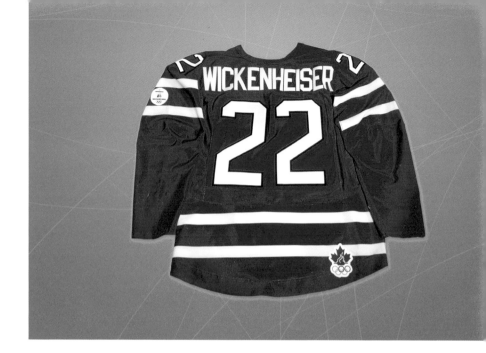

WOMEN'S HOCKEY AT THE OLYMPICS

A Team Canada veteran and five-time Olympic medallist, Hayley Wickenheiser plays leadership roles on and off the ice, inspiring young players to make a difference in the world.

Wickenheiser wore these skates and this jersey as captain of the Canadian women's national team. The team won gold at the 2010 Winter Olympics.

WICKENHEISER'S JERSEY

Worn in Vancouver, B.C.
2010

WICKENHEISER'S SKATES

Worn in Vancouver, B.C.
2010

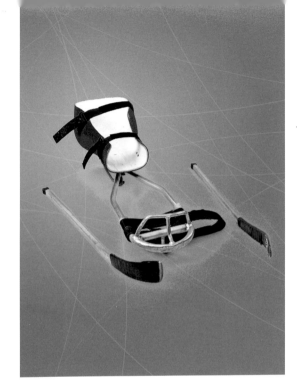

MELLWAY'S HOCKEY SLEDGE AND STICKS

Designed and built
by Canwin Sports
Ottawa, Ont.
Around 2000

AN ADAPTIVE SPORT

Sledge hockey is a version of the sport designed for players who have a lower body disability. The rules are the same as hockey, but players' sticks and skates have been adapted. Dean Mellway is a sledge hockey pioneer. He used this sledge, designed and built by the company he founded with teammate Lou Mulvihill, for international competition.

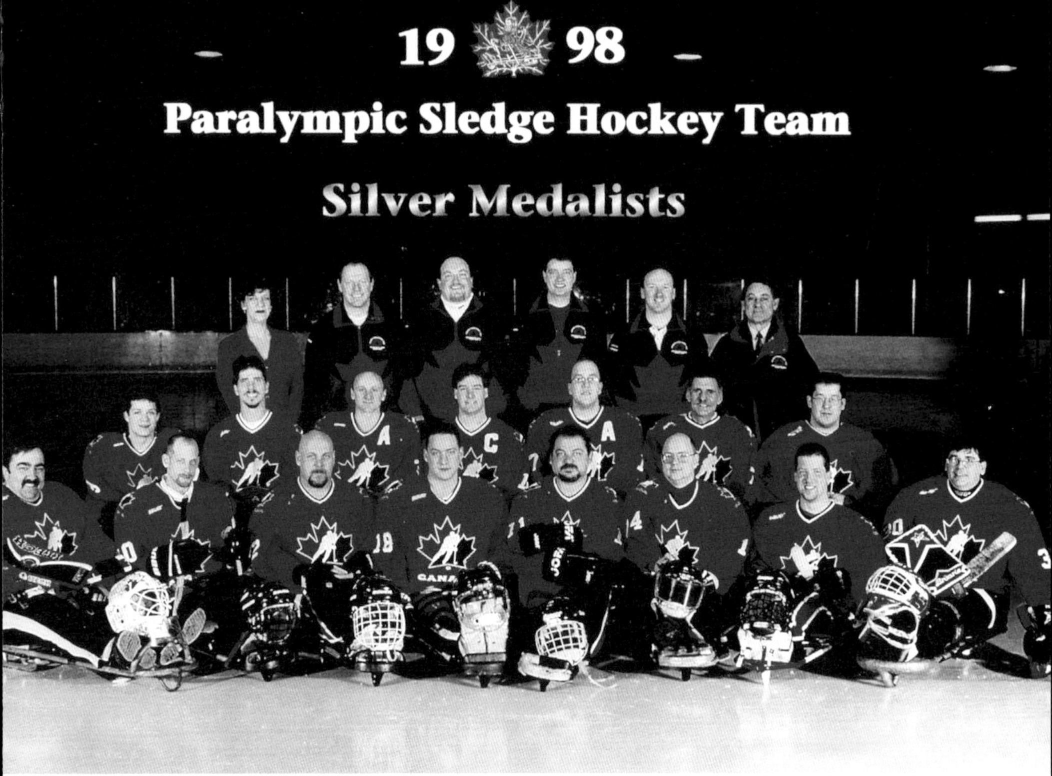
19 98
Paralympic Sledge Hockey Team
Silver Medalists

▲

TEAM CANADA

Dean Mellway (second row, second from right)
Nagano Winter Paralympics, 1998

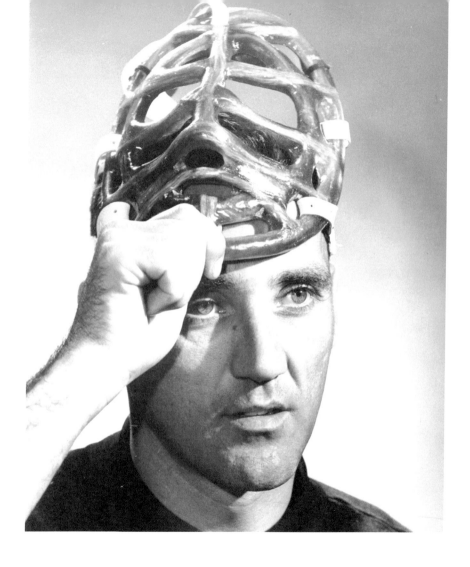

STOPPING THE PUCK

The goalie plays hockey's most specialized position and is the key to team defence. Goalie equipment has become more extensive and more complex as the sport itself has become faster and more dangerous.

Masks, which goalies often personalize with designs and messages, are the most visible example. Leg pads have become larger and lighter too, and there is additional protection for the neck, midsection and forearms. When dressed to play, the modern goaltender looks like an ancient armoured warrior.

**JACQUES PLANTE
LIFTING HIS HOCKEY MASK**

1960

CHANGING THE FACE OF THE GAME

This was Jacques Plante's third mask, worn in 1963 while he played with the New York Rangers. The fibreglass strands made the mask lighter and cooler than the original, solid mask.

PLANTE'S MASK

Designed by W. A. Burchmore and E. T. P. Greenland
Early 1960s
Fibreglass

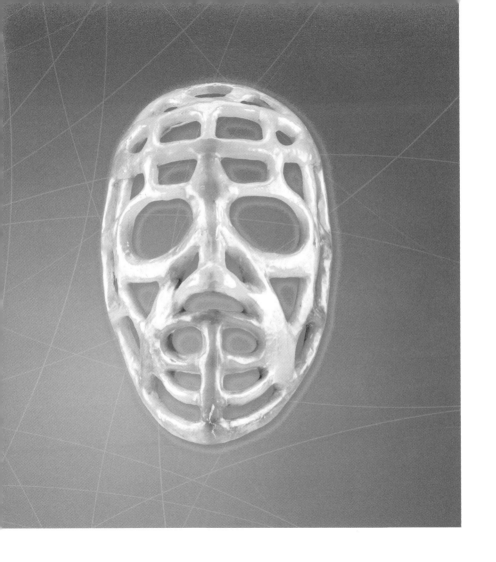

The Hockey Sweater

Story by
Roch Carrier

Illustrations by
Sheldon Cohen

WEARING TEAM COLOURS

The hockey sweater and jacket are emblems
of belonging, whether worn by team members
or by fans. Team colours and logos are
instantly recognizable — Toronto Maple Leafs
blue, for example, or the red, white and blue
of the Montréal Canadiens. They are sources
of immense pride and identity, as well as
lucrative corporate sales.

The earliest hockey sweaters were woollen
home-knits. Modern jerseys range from
inexpensive synthetics to exact replicas
of those worn by the professionals.

THE HOCKEY SWEATER

Roch Carrier
1979

**PRICE'S
MONTRÉAL
CANADIENS
JERSEY**

2014–2015 season

HOCKEY HEROES

Carey Price, who worked with young people through the Breakfast Club of Canada, schools and youth sports, won the Jean Béliveau trophy for community service in 2014. He and his team wore jerseys displaying the number 4 during that season as a tribute to Béliveau.

**CROSBY'S
PITTSBURGH
PENGUINS
JERSEY**

2015

THE FACE OF THE NHL

Sidney Crosby has made it big in the NHL, while staying true to his hometown values. His star power has made the colours and logo of the Pittsburgh Penguins instantly recognizable to contemporary hockey fans in Canada.

THE 1972 SUMMIT SERIES

Many Canadians recall Paul Henderson's final
goal in the 1972 Summit Series against the
Soviet team as an iconic moment, perhaps
even *the* iconic moment, in the history of
Canadian sports.

HENDERSON'S SUMMIT SERIES JERSEY

Worn in Moscow,
U.S.S.R.
1972

**CROSBY'S
OLYMPIC JERSEY**

Worn in Vancouver, B.C.
2010

THE GOLDEN GOAL

Crosby wore this jersey while playing for Team Canada at the Winter Olympics in Vancouver. On February 28, 2010, millions of Canadians celebrated his overtime goal, which won Canada a gold medal.

THE TEAM
BEHIND
THE TEAM

////////////////////////

Whether at the elite level or at
the neighbourhood rink, the work
accomplished by the team behind
the team has an important impact
on the players' on-ice performance.

ON SORT UN GARS
DE LA POLICE,
MAIS ON SORT PAS
LA POLICE DU GARS.

A LEGENDARY COACH

Pat Burns once said that coaching is the toughest job in hockey. In 1983, superstar Wayne Gretzky hired Burns, a Gatineau police officer and part-time coach, as head coach of the Hull (now Gatineau) Olympiques. Burns would become a hockey legend.

In Montréal, he became a well-known public figure. He also coached in Toronto and Boston, and won the Stanley Cup with the New Jersey Devils.

PAT BURNS, 1990

Serge Chapleau (1945–)

COACH'S WHISTLE

Used by Burns
1990s

STANLEY CUP-WINNING TIE

Worn by Burns, Head Coach, New Jersey Devils
June 9, 2003

BURNS' POLICE BADGE

Gatineau, Que.
1970 to 1986

AN IMPACT PLAYER

Jacques Demers began coaching professional hockey in 1975. While with Detroit, he was twice NHL Coach of the Year; with Montréal, he won the Stanley Cup in 1993.

JACQUES DEMERS

Head Coach of the Montréal Canadiens
1992

LLOYD PERCIVAL

Fitness expert
1972

COACHING ATHLETES

When Lloyd Percival published *The Hockey Handbook* in 1951, few hockey players used his training techniques and dietary methods. Today, his advice is both accepted and commonplace.

A COMMUNITY RAISES A PLAYER

Hockey players, who benefit from local support networks, make it their business to give back to communities. From the moment they first step on the ice, their success is actively encouraged by those around them. When they do well, the whole community celebrates.

JEAN-GABRIEL
PAGEAU VISITING
A HOSPITAL

Gatineau, Que.
2011

FOR THE LOVE
OF THE GAME

////////////////////////

Hockey fans share their love of the
game. Whether they follow elite-
level teams or minor league players,
they cheer madly at game results
and wear team colours. Some even
produce homemade products with
team logos.

HOCKEY MEMORABILIA

Before social media allowed fans to share information online, people kept scrapbooks of newspaper clippings and memorabilia of their favourite players.

By choosing to wear clothing and carry items decorated with the colours and images of their favourite team or player, fans bring the joy of the game into their everyday lives. Sometimes, they hang on to childhood mementoes into their adult years.

CLOCKWISE FROM UPPER LEFT:

Calgary Inferno cap, Bobby Orr lunch box, Maurice "Rocket" Richard licence plate, Wayne Gretzky lunch box, Maurice Richard jacket, O-Pee-Chee chewing gum wrappers

SUBBAN SIGNING
WINTER CLASSIC JERSEY

SOCIAL MEDIA FANDOM

Today, fans get a behind-the-scenes look at the NHL thanks to social media-savvy players like P. K. Subban. He uses hashtags like #pkapproved and #belikePK to engage fans and raise awareness of social issues.

FROM PHOTOGRAPH
TO ICONIC IMAGE

In 1934, BeeHive introduced a photographic series featuring hockey players to promote its corn syrup. The photo of Charlie Conacher of the Toronto Maple Leafs (page 78) later reappeared as a motif in Canadian art and commercial design.

CHARLIE
CONACHER

1934

MARY MAXIM HOCKEY SWEATER AND PATTERN

Around 1960

HOCKEY FAN COLLECTIONS

Like all collectors, Mike Wilson, known as "The Ultimate Leafs Fan," loves to gather and share the stories behind each of the gems in his collection.

TORONTO MAPLE LEAFS BOBBLE-HEAD DOLL

Toronto, Ont.
1960s

YORK PEANUT BUTTER PROMO TUMBLER

Toronto, Ont.
1960

MAPLE LEAF GARDENS OPENING NIGHT PROGRAM

Toronto, Ont.
November 12, 1931

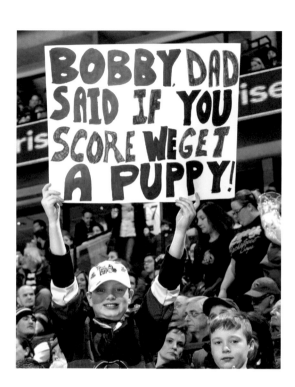

YOUNG FANS ENCOURAGING OTTAWA SENATORS FORWARD BOBBY RYAN

Ottawa, Ont.
2016

THE GOAL THAT SCORED A DOG

On January 24, 2016, the Jansen-Kirkwood family held up this sign at the Ottawa Senators game, encouraging Bobby Ryan to score a goal. And it worked! Their new puppy's name is Bobby.

MAURICE
"ROCKET"
RICHARD
SOUP CAN

Montréal, Que
1955

THE RICHARD RIOT

Montréal hockey fans rioted on March 17, 1955, after Maurice Richard was suspended by NHL President Clarence Campbell. Fans who boycotted the Campbell soup brand, mistakenly associating it with the League president, could purchase this specially canned "Rocket" Richard soup instead.

WE WIN… WE CELEBRATE…

Serge Chapleau (1945–)
Montréal, Que.
1986
Ink on card

HOARDING WALL

Vancouver, B.C.
June 15, 2011

VANCOUVER RIOT

In 2011, rioting broke out in Vancouver after the Boston Bruins defeated the hometown Canucks in the Stanley Cup finals. The next day, fans cleared the streets downtown. Plywood covering boarded-up windows became a place for people to share their thoughts on the violent events.

HOCKEY MAKES HEADLINES

////////////////////

The business of hockey is big news. From the earliest days of the amateur and professional leagues, journalists on the beat have kept the public informed of the hiring and firing of coaches, player trades, strikes and lockouts, and financial deals.

SUMMIT SERIES STAR PAUL HENDERSON
READING THE HEADLINES

1972

GROWTH OF THE NHL

The NHL was established in 1917, with just four
Canadian teams. For the 2017–2018 season, the
league will have 31 teams located throughout
North America. Each announcement about the
NHL's expansion is headline news.

**OFFICIAL NHL
HOCKEY PUCKS**

1990s

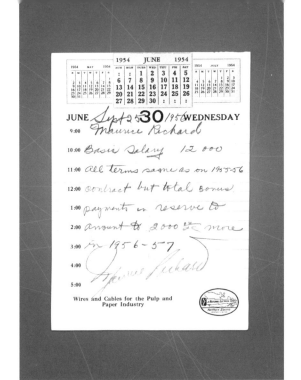

**HOCKEY HALL
OF FAME
INDUCTION RING**

Given to Foster Hewitt
1965

**CONTRACT
BETWEEN
MAURICE
"ROCKET"
RICHARD AND
THE MONTRÉAL
CANADIENS**

1956

THE CONTRACT

The National Hockey League Players' Association, formed in 1966,
demanded revisions to the standard contracts then in use. Today,
collectors seek early contracts like this one as reminders of how
the game has changed.

THE VOICE OF "HOCKEY NIGHT IN CANADA"

Long-time fans remember Foster Hewitt as the voice of the English-
language radio program "Hockey Night in Canada" in the 1930s. He made
the transition to television in 1952, when the show was first televised.
In French Canada, René Lecavalier was the iconic voice of "La Soirée
du hockey."

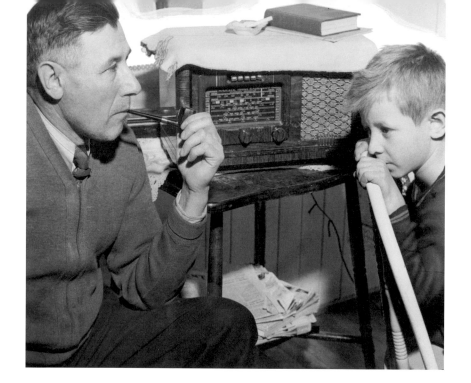

**FATHER AND SON LISTENING TO A
"HOCKEY NIGHT IN CANADA" RADIO BROADCAST**

Around 1936

VANCOUVER 2010

Marie-Philip Poulin scored the game-winning goal in the women's gold medal match between Canada and the United States at the 2010 Winter Olympics.

POULIN SCORES IN THE GOLD MEDAL MATCH

Vancouver Winter Olympics, 2010

PASSION FOR THE GAME

///////////////////////

Featured in art, literature, music and even comic books, hockey is part of the Canadian cultural landscape, evidence of the deep meaning and relevance of the game to Canadians.

THE ROCKET SCORES

In this painting, artist Saul Miller depicts Maurice "Rocket" Richard as a religious icon. The opposing Toronto Maple Leafs are clumsy barnyard animals, and the referees become the Blind Mice of nursery rhymes.

THE ROCKET SCORES

Saul Miller (1942–)
1998
Acrylic on canvas

THE HOCKEY PLAYER

Known for his distinctive expressionist style and depictions of urban Indigenous experiences, Clifford Maracle uses bold colour in this painting to reflect the strength and speed of the hockey player in motion.

THE HOCKEY PLAYER

Clifford Maracle
(1944–1996)
Mohawk, 1974
Acrylic on canvas

PORTRAIT OF A PLAYER

CASSIE CAMPBELL

Bryan Adams (1959–)
1999
Silver gelatin print on
aluminum

As captain of Team Canada, Cassie Campbell-
Pascall won two Olympic gold medals. She
is now a commentator with CBC Sports.
Musician and photographer Bryan Adams
took this portrait.

SHANIA TWAIN

Singer Shania Twain hosted the 2003 Juno Awards wearing clothing inspired by NHL team sweaters. Her only outfit sporting a number was inspired by the Montréal Canadiens and featured Maurice Richard's #9.

TWAIN'S #9 OUTFIT

Worn in Ottawa, Ont.
2003

COMMUNITY PRIDE

The Pikangikum Winterhawks, a hockey powerhouse in Northern Ontario throughout the 1980s, were the source of enormous community pride. The team's logo is beaded onto these mittens.

PIKANGIKUM WINTERHAWKS MITTENS

Attributed to
Noreen Peters
Ojibwa/Anishinabe,
1980s
Beads and leather

RURAL POND HOCKEY

Lytton, B.C.
2010

A PASSION FOR PLAY

Hockey is part of people's everyday lives. Street and pond hockey are known to most Canadian children, as are sock hockey and floor hockey, shinny and pickup, ball hockey and sledge hockey. There is even underwater hockey.

The sport has inspired board games and arcade games, as well as tabletop hockey, air hockey and dozens of electronic games. There are also hockey-themed toys, novelties and collectibles. In all its variants, hockey is fun!

TABLETOP HOCKEY

During the Depression, Don H. Munro of Burlington, Ontario, built a table-based hockey game for his family, using materials around his home. Adapting this idea, Canadian company Eagle Toys made the game we know today.

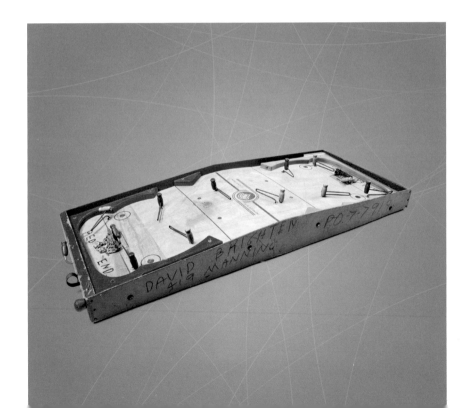

**EARLY TABLE
HOCKEY GAME**

Produced by Munro Games
Around 1940

**PEE-WEE TABLE
HOCKEY GAME**

Produced by Eagle Toys Ltd.
1960

HERB CARNEGIE OF THE QUEBEC ACES

1953

GAME CHANGERS

Individuals have used the sport to help change society, respond to injustice and engage with the general public. Like other competitive sports, hockey has not always responded well to diversity and social change.

Players, coaches, fans and family members inspired by community issues or personal experience have led some of the sport's most far-reaching initiatives. Whether through youth camps — like the one initiated by Herb Carnegie — or in coming forward to speak out against homophobia and sexism, athletes have made an impact.

HERBIE
CARNEGIE

BLAINEY'S HOCKEY TROPHY (RIGHT)

1987

CHAPLEAU'S HOCKEY TROPHY (LEFT), BADGES AND BUTTON

1979, 1980s

CHARTER CHALLENGE

In 1986, an Ontario Human Rights tribunal found that rules preventing Justine Blainey from playing hockey with boys contravened the Canadian Charter of Rights and Freedoms. The only female member of her team, Justine won this trophy in 1987.

WOMEN'S HOCKEY HONOURS

In 1982, player-organizer Manon Chapleau ensured that Quebec was represented at the first annual Abby Hoffman Cup, which took place in Brampton, Ontario. She kept these souvenirs of her hockey career.

JUSTINE BLAINEY, 13, AFTER WINNING HER BID TO PLAY ON A BOYS' TEAM

Toronto, Ont.
1986

**MANON
CHAPLEAU OF
THE MONTRÉAL
TITANS**

1979–1980 season

HOCKEY'S FLYING FATHERS

1982

FLYING FATHERS

In 1963, a group of Roman Catholic priests played their first hockey game as the Flying Fathers. Over the next 40 years, they toured North America, drawing laughs and raising millions for local charities.

HOMETOWN HOCKEY

Hockey is a community pursuit, with close ties between town and team. The sport helps create local pride, civic spirit and community traditions.

Teams and stadiums become the focus of major events, fundraisers and volunteer efforts. In town rinks, people vote, attend bake sales, give blood or attend public information sessions. Arena closures always spark a major debate, and arena upgrading is a reason to celebrate.

FANS CHEERING

Ottawa Senators vs. Buffalo Sabres
J. L. Grightmire Arena, Dundas, Ont.
2010

///////////////////////////////

**Hockey is Canada's national
conversation starter:
"How about that game?"**

///////////////////////////////

CONTRIBUTIONS

////////////////////////////

Full credit goes to the group of talented individuals who contributed to making this exhibition a success. They gave 110%, proving that a solid team effort makes good things happen.

A special thanks to Dominique Savard, Sophie Doucet, Martine Seewaldt, France Therrien, Erin Gurski and Dean Oliver for their expertise and collegiality. The creative design is thanks to Groupe GID Design, Chantal Baril and Nadine Marsolais. We are also grateful to Daniel Pellerin, Mélissa Duncan and Joe Pelletier for their research contributions.

This souvenir catalogue owes its production to Publications Coordinator Lee Wyndham and to Photographer Steven Darby.

We would like to acknowledge the individuals and institutions that loaned artifacts, supplied images and directed us to important sources, enriching the exhibition and this catalogue. A huge thank you to colleagues at the Canadian Museum of History, and throughout the country, for sharing your personal hockey memories, photographs and opinions. We enjoyed working with you!

PHOTO CREDITS

CANADIAN MUSEUM OF HISTORY

p. 5	IMG2015-0039-0007-Dm / Steven Darby
p. 13	IMG2016-0253-0026-Dm / Steven Darby
p. 14	IMG2016-0253-0001-Dm / Steven Darby
p. 15	IMG2016-0253-0002-Dm / Steven Darby
p. 16	IMG2016-0253-0039-Dm / Steven Darby
p. 22	IMG2016-0253-0011-Dm / Steven Darby
p. 28	IMG2016-0253-0021-Dm / Steven Darby
p. 30	19840238-001, 19840238-001a
p. 36	IMG2016-0253-0012-Dm / Steven Darby
p. 39	IMG2016-0073-0002-Dm / Steven Darby
p. 43	IMG2016-0253-0025-Dm / Steven Darby
p. 47	IMG2016-0253-0038-Dm / Steven Darby
p. 48	IMG2016-0253-0004-Dm / Steven Darby
p. 49	IMG2016-0253-0037-Dm / Steven Darby
p. 50	IMG2016-0253-0032-Dm / Steven Darby
p. 51	IMG2016-0197-0001-Dm / James MacCulloch
p. 55	IMG2009-0063-0044-Dm / Marie-Louise Deruaz
p. 58	IMG2016-0253-0018-Dm / Steven Darby
p. 59	IMG2016-0253-0016-Dm / Steven Darby
p. 60	IMG2016-0253-0046-Dm / Steven Darby
p. 61	IMG2016-0253-0049-Dm / Steven Darby
p. 67	IMG2016-0253-0013-Dm / Private collection, Burns family
p. 74	IMG2016-0253-0034-Dm / Steven Darby
p. 78	IMG2014-0143-003-Dm
p. 79	IMG2016-0253-0041-Dm / Steven Darby
p. 80	IMG2016-0253-0052-Dm / Steven Darby / Private collection, Mike Wilson, "The Ultimate Leafs Fan"
p. 83	IMG2009-0192-0008-Dm / Harry Foster
p. 85	IMG2016-0253-0005-Dm / Steven Darby
p. 89	IMG2016-0253-0044-Dm / Steven Darby
p. 90	IMG2016-0253-0033-Dm / Steven Darby
p. 91	IMG2016-0253-0035-Dm / Steven Darby
p. 96	IMG2009-0231-0001-Dm / Harry Foster
p. 98	IMG2016-0253-0045-Dm / Steven Darby
p. 100	IMG2016-0253-0008-Dm / Steven Darby
p. 101	IMG2016-0253-0042-Dm / Steven Darby
p. 104	IMG2016-0253-0006-Dm / Steven Darby
p. 105	IMG2016-0253-0030-Dm / Steven Darby
p. 108	IMG2016-0253-0040-Dm / Steven Darby

EXTERNAL SOURCES

p. 6	Getty Images / Photo by Bruce Bennett
p. 9	© 6okean / Adobe Stock / 100638433
p. 11	Library and Archives Canada / e011165573
p. 19	Notman & Son / Library and Archives Canada / e011184848
p. 20	Thomas Allan & Co. / M976.188.1 / McCord Museum, Montréal
p. 23	William James Topley / Library and Archives Canada / a025686

p. 25 J. E. Livernois / Library and Archives Canada / e011184877

p. 26 Library and Archives Canada / e010965429,30,35,39,44,45

p. 29 City of Cambridge Archives Photograph Collection

p. 31 Library and Archives Canada / e011161364

p. 32 Courtesy of the City of Toronto Archives

p. 35 Getty Images / Photo by Jana Chytilova

p. 37 Bibliothèque et Archives nationales du Québec / P1000,D1132,P8

p. 41 © Lorraine Swanson / Adobe Stock / 73374108

p. 44 York University Libraries, Clara Thomas Archives & Special Collections, Toronto Telegram fonds, ASC08456

p. 46 T. Eaton Co. Limited / Library and Archives Canada / e011189600 / © Sears Canada Inc.h

p. 52 Library and Archives Canada / e010933903

p. 56 Used by permission of Tundra Books, a division of Penguin Random House Canada Ltd.

p. 63 © iofoto / Adobe Stock / 5265506

p. 64 M996.10.208 / Pat Burns / Serge Chapleau / McCord Museum, Montréal

p. 68 Getty Images / National Hockey League / Photo by Denis Brodeur

p. 70 Getty Images / *Toronto Star* / Photo by Fred Ross

p. 71 *Le Droit* / Photo by Patrick Woodbury

p. 72 Getty Images / Getty Image Sport / Dylan Lynch

p. 76 Lotus Photography

p. 82 Getty Images / Photo by Jana Chytilova

p. 84 M996.10.308 / Serge Chapleau / McCord Museum, Montréal

p. 87 © maxcam / Adobe Stock / 79579529

p. 88 Getty Images / *Toronto Star* / Photo by Boris Spremo

p. 92 Glenbow Archives

p. 93 Getty Images / *Toronto Star* / Photo by Rick Madonik

p. 95 Roth and Ramberg Photography Inc.

p. 99 Library and Archives Canada / e010752920 / Photo by Bryan Adams

p. 102 Photo by Bernie Fandrich

p. 107 *La Patrie*

p. 110 Getty Images / *Toronto Star* / Photo by Andrew Stawicki

p. 111 Courtesy of Manon Chapleau

p. 112 Getty Images / *Toronto Star* / Photo by Pat Brennan

p. 115 Peter Power / *The Globe and Mail*